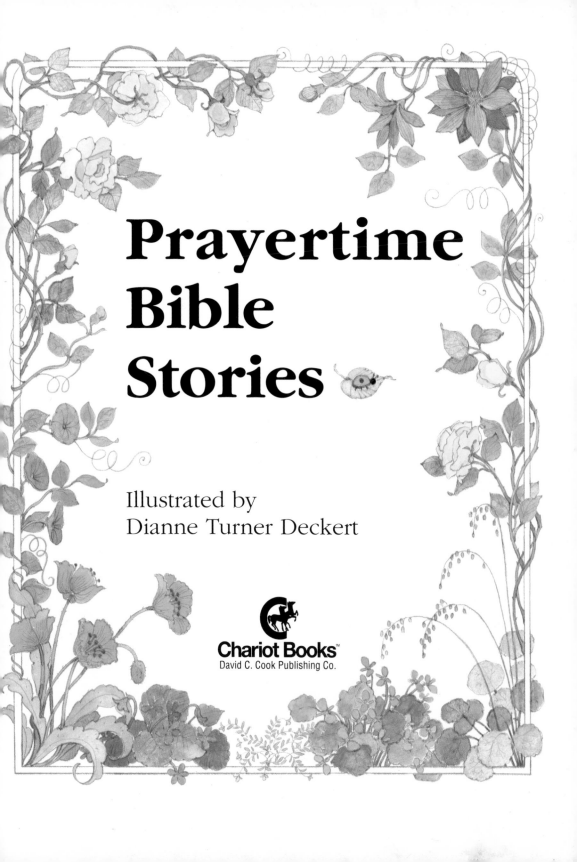

Prayertime Bible Stories

Illustrated by
Dianne Turner Deckert

Chariot Books™
David C. Cook Publishing Co.

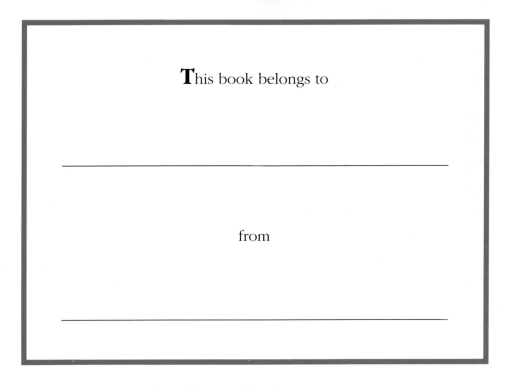

This book belongs to

_____

from

_____

Chariot Books™ is an imprint of David C. Cook Publishing Co.
David C. Cook Publishing Co., Elgin, IL 60120
David C. Cook Publishing Co., Weston, Ontario
Nova Distributors, Ltd., Torquay, England

PRAYERTIME BIBLE STORIES

Edited by Jeannie Harmon
Cover and internal design by Nancy L. Haskins

First printing, 1992
Printed in Singapore
96 95 94 93 92 5 4 3 2 1

Library of Congress Cataloging-in-Publication Data

Prayertime Bible Stories / illustrated by Dianne Turner Deckert.
        p.   cm.
  Summary: Presents a collection of Bible stories from both the Old
and New Testaments, each followed by review questions and a prayer.
  ISBN 0-7814-0045-7
  1. Bible stories, English. 2. Children–Prayer-books and
devotions–English. [1. Bible stories. 2. Prayer books and
devotions.] I. Deckert, Dianne Turner, ill. II. Title: Prayer
time Bible stories.
  BS551.2P73 1992
  220.9'505–dc20
                                                            91-35647
                                                                CIP
                                                                 AC

Table of Contents

And God Said, "That's Good!"

In the beginning there was no earth, no sky, no sun, no moon, and no people. There was only God.

God made everything by the power of His word. When He said something, it happened!

On the first day, God said, "Let there be light," and there was light. He called the light "day," and the darkness "night."

"That's good," He said.

On the second day, God said, "Let the water be separated from the sky above." Beautiful blue sky appeared and the air was clean and pure.

"That's good," He said.

Then God spoke and the waters came together into seas, and dry land appeared. There was dirt and rocks and clay, but nothing grew on the earth. So God said, "Let the land become alive with plants and trees, flowers and grass."

All this God did on the third day, and He said, "That's good."

On the fourth day, God said, "Let stars and a moon shine at night, and a sun shine during the day. Let there be seasons – summer, fall, winter, spring – and days, months, and years."

And God said, "That's good."

"Let there be fish in the water and birds in the sky. And let them each have babies to keep their kind going." And God looked at the work He had done on the fifth day and said, "That's good."

All the animals were created on the sixth day. Then God decided to create people — beings like Himself — who could take care of all of His creation. So God made Adam and Eve in His own image. He blessed them and told them to have children so there would be people all over the world. And He gave them fruits and vegetables and grains for their food.

God looked at everything He had made and said, "That's very good. I think I'll take a rest."

So on the seventh day, God rested from all His work.

Story based on Genesis 1—2:3.

❖ *What are some things God made?*

❖ *What did God say when He finished His work?*

Prayer:
Thank You, God, for making such a wonderful world.
Help me to take care of all the things You've given
me to enjoy. Amen.

The Snake Who Told a Lie

Adam and Eve lived in the Garden of Eden—the most beautiful garden in all the world. God placed them in the garden to take care of it and enjoy its beauty. But God had one rule.

"You can eat from any tree in the garden," God said, "but you must not eat from the tree of the knowledge of good and evil. If you eat from this tree, you will surely die."

One day as Eve was walking in the garden, she came to this special tree. A snake spoke to her. "Has God told you that you may not eat the fruit from this tree?" the snake asked.

"We may eat from every tree but this one," Eve said. "If we eat from this one, God said we would die."

"You won't die," the snake said. "If you eat the fruit, you will be wise like God, knowing good and evil."

Eve looked at the fruit. It looked so delicious. She decided to taste it. "I must give some to Adam," she said. She did, and Adam ate it, too.

Suddenly Adam and Eve were afraid. They ran and hid because they knew they had disobeyed God.

But God called to Adam. "Where are you?"

Adam said, "When we heard You in the garden, we were afraid. So we hid in the trees."

"Have you eaten the fruit I told you not to eat?" God asked.

"Eve gave it to me," Adam said, trying to blame her.

"The snake told me to eat it," Eve said, trying to blame the snake.

God would not *make* them obey. Adam and Eve chose to believe the lie of a snake, instead of being obedient to God. He had to punish them for disobeying Him.

"You must leave the garden I made for you," God said. "You must go out and work hard for your food."

So Adam and Eve left the garden. On the path God placed an angel with a sword of fire. Adam and Eve could never go back again!

Story based on Genesis 2 and 3.

❖ *What lie did the snake tell Eve?*

❖ *Does God make you obey His Word? How do you know?*

Prayer:
Dear Lord, help me make the wise choice to obey Your Word.

Amen.

The Animal Ark Hotel

God was very sad. The world He had made was beautiful, but the people He had created did not obey Him. They wanted to do evil things.

"Why should we work?" they said. "We'll steal what we want from our neighbors."

"The sun makes our crops grow," they said. "So let's worship the sun instead of God."

Finally, God said, "I will destroy all of the people, the animals, and the birds. I am sorry that I made them."

But there was one good family that God did not want to destroy—Noah's family. One day God said to Noah, "I will send a flood to cover the earth. You must make a boat. It will keep you and your family safe."

So Noah began to build the ark. He followed God's plan exactly.

The wicked people laughed at Noah. "Poor Noah thinks he can float a boat on dry land," they said.

But Noah went right on doing what God told him to do. At last the ark was finished. Again God spoke to Noah, "Go into the ark. Take seven pairs of animals and birds that are good to eat. Take one pair of each kind that is not good to eat."

It was a big job getting all the animals into the ark. Elephants, giraffes, zebras, hippos—every one had a special spot to eat and sleep. The ark was one BIG animal hotel! When all were inside, God shut the door.

It began to rain. It rained for forty days and forty nights. Water covered the whole earth. But everyone in the ark was safe.

At last the rain stopped. The water went down. God told Noah that his family and the animals could come out of the ark. The birds stretched their wings and flew. The animals pushed and ran to reach the new green grass.

Noah and his family built an altar to worship God for keeping them safe.

God was pleased with Noah. "I will never again send water to cover the earth," God said. Then God put a beautiful rainbow in the sky. "When you see a rainbow, remember My promise," God said. And God has never broken His promise.

Story based on Genesis 6:1—9:17.

❖ *Why did God want to destroy what He had made?*

❖ *What are some animals that could have been in the animal hotel?*

Prayer:
Dear Lord, help me to always obey You.
And thanks, God, for keeping me safe.

Amen.

9

Brother For Sale

Jacob had twelve sons, but Joseph was his favorite. Jacob loved Joseph so much that he made him a beautiful coat of many colors.

One day Joseph's brothers were far from home taking care of their father's sheep. When they talked about Joseph, they became angry.

"Why doesn't Joseph work as hard as we do? Why doesn't Father give us beautiful coats like the one he gave Joseph?" they asked. All at once one of the brothers pointed across the field.

"Look!" he cried. "Here comes Joseph. He is probably coming to spy on us."

"Let's get rid of him," one of the brothers said. "We will tell Father a wild animal killed him."

So when Joseph reached his brothers, they grabbed him and took off his beautiful coat and threw him into a pit.

"Please don't!" Joseph cried. "I have done nothing wrong. Father sent me. . . ." But his brothers wouldn't listen to his cries.

The pit was wet and dark. He must have been scared to be in the pit alone, but God was there with him.

Some traders came along and Joseph's brothers sold him for twenty pieces of silver. He was taken far, far away to the land of Egypt. There, the traders sold Joseph as a slave.

He worked very hard for his master. He trusted God to help him do his work well and God blessed all that Joseph did.

Many years later, Joseph's brothers were starving. There was little food in the land of Israel, so the brothers came to Egypt to buy grain. They did not realize the one from whom they bought the grain was their brother Joseph. When Joseph told his brothers who he was, they were afraid he would kill them. But instead, he forgave them.

"Don't be afraid," Joseph said. "You sold me as a slave to hurt me, but God wanted me to come to Egypt to save you from hunger."

Joseph trusted God, and God helped Joseph to become a mighty ruler in Egypt.

Story based on Genesis 37, 39, and 45.

❖ *Why did Joseph's brothers want to kill him?*

❖ *How did Joseph treat his brothers when they came to Egypt to buy food?*

Prayer:
Dear Lord, help me remember when people are mean to me, You still love me and will help me.

Amen.

The Boy with the Powerful Sling

The Israelites waited for the battle to begin. Their enemies the Philistines were camped across the valley. Suddenly, a tall giant appeared from the Philistine camp. His name was Goliath.

He shouted across the valley, "Send a man to fight me. If he kills me, the Philistines will leave. If I kill him, you will be our slaves."

For forty days and forty nights the giant called to the Israelites. King Saul and his armies were terrified.

Then one day a young shepherd boy named David was watching his father's sheep near Bethlehem.

"Take some food to your brothers, David," his father said. "Then come and tell me about the battle."

When David reached the camp of the Israelites, he asked, "How is the battle going?"

Suddenly Goliath shouted and the Israelite soldiers ran in fear.

David looked about in surprise. "Why doesn't someone go out to fight this man?" asked David.

"Be quiet," one of his brothers said. "No man can fight that giant."

But David wouldn't be quiet. "Don't be afraid," he said. "I'll fight the giant."

When King Saul heard this, he put his big suit of armor on David.

"I can't fight with your armor," said David. "I must fight the way I know how, with my sling and God's help." So David took his sling and five smooth stones from a nearby stream, and went to face Goliath.

Goliath was angry. "Am I a dog that a boy comes out to fight me?"

David said, "You come to me with a sword and a spear, but I come to you in the name of the Lord."

David quickly ran to meet the giant. He put a stone in his sling and whirled it 'round and 'round. The stone flew through the air and hit Goliath in the forehead. The giant fell to the ground. David took the giant's sword and cut Goliath's head off. When the Philistines saw that their hero was dead, they turned and ran. Israel was free from the Philistines.

Story based on I Samuel 17.

❖ *How many stones did it take to knock the giant down?*

❖ *Why was David not afraid to fight the giant?*

Prayer:
Your Word—the Bible—tells me that You will give me strength in times of trouble. Thank You, God, for always being there when I need help. Amen.

Is Your God Sleeping?

Ahab was a wicked king. He did not love God. Instead, he worshiped the idol Baal. His wife, Jezebel, was also very wicked. She ordered soldiers to put God's prophet Elijah to death. But no one could find him.

Finally, Elijah sent a challenge to Ahab. "Tell the 450 priests of Baal and all the people to come to Mt. Carmel."

King Ahab was afraid because he knew Elijah was a man of God. So he did what Elijah said.

At Mt. Carmel, Elijah stood in front of all the people. "How long will you try to worship two gods?" he asked. "If our God is really the true God, you should worship Him. If Baal is the true God, worship him.

"Today we'll have a test," he said. "Let the priests of Baal put some meat on an altar. I will put meat on a different altar. The priests can call on the name of their god, and I will call on the name of the Lord. The god who answers by burning up the meat is the true God."

The people nodded their heads. "This is a good test," they said.

The priests of Baal danced around their altar and shouted, "O Baal, answer us!" They cried louder and louder for Baal to hear them. But there was no fire.

"Maybe your god is sleeping or taking a vacation," Elijah said. "Shout louder!"

They shouted and danced around their sacrifice all day. But still there was no fire.

Then Elijah built an altar with twelve big stones and put big pieces of meat on it. He ordered the people to pour water on it three times. Everything was soaked. Finally, Elijah prayed. "O God, let these people know that You are God."

Suddenly fire flashed down from the sky. It burned up the meat, the wood, and the twelve stones.

The people fell with their faces to the ground and shouted, "The Lord is our God! We will serve Him!"

Story based on I Kings 17 and 18.

❖ *What did the prophets of Baal do to get their god's attention?*

❖ *How did God show that He was the one true God?*

Prayer:
O Lord, please help me to worship
and obey You even when it seems like
everyone else has forgotten You.

Amen.

The Prophet Who Had Seaweed for Lunch

God's people couldn't make up their minds—sometimes they obeyed His law and sometimes they did not. Because God never stopped loving them, He sent prophets to remind the people to obey His ways.

One day God spoke to Jonah the prophet. "Go to Nineveh," He said. "Tell the people to stop doing wrong or their city will be destroyed."

Jonah was afraid to go to Nineveh. It was a wicked city, and the Assyrian soldiers who lived there were strong and very cruel.

"The people are wicked; they should be destroyed," Jonah said to himself. So, instead of doing what God told him to do, Jonah ran away. He got on a ship that was going to Tarshish, far away from Nineveh.

While the ship was at sea, a terrible storm came up. The sailors were afraid. "What can we do?" they cried.

Jonah knew that the storm had come because he was running away from God. "It's my fault," he said. "Throw me into the sea."

The sailors did, and a big fish swallowed Jonah. For three days Jonah lived in the stomach of the fish. He had nothing to eat. His only choice was to have seaweed for lunch! Finally, God made the fish cast Jonah up on the shore. Then He spoke to Jonah again. "Go to Nineveh. Tell the people to stop doing wrong or their city will be destroyed."

This time Jonah did not run away. Instead he decided to obey God.

Jonah went to Nineveh and told the people: "You must change your ways or your city will be destroyed in forty days."

The people were afraid. They ran to the king and told him what Jonah had said.

"Jonah is right," the king said. "We must stop being mean and selfish. We must pray to God and ask Him to forgive us."

The people were sorry; they asked God to forgive them and help them do right. He did not destroy the city.

Story based on the Book of Jonah.

❖ *Why didn't Jonah want to go to Nineveh?*

❖ *How did God teach Jonah to obey?*

Prayer:
Lord, thank You for teaching us how we should live. Help me to remember to obey Your Word and those who take care of me.   Amen.

The Lions Lost Their Dinner!

Daniel was honest and always did the right thing. So King Darius put Daniel in charge of all the princes of Babylon. This made the princes very mad. They planned how they could get rid of Daniel.

"If Daniel would do something wrong," they said, "then we could trap him."

But Daniel didn't do wrong things. He always asked God to show him what to do. He prayed to God three times each day.

One day the princes came up with an idea. "King Darius," they said, "make a law that everyone must worship only you for thirty days. Whoever does not will be thrown into a den of lions."

The king, who liked Daniel, did not know the princes were trying to trap Daniel. So he signed the law.

The next day when Daniel prayed to God, the princes listened at his door. They knew Daniel would only worship the One true God. They quickly ran to tell the king what they heard.

The king was sorry he made the foolish law. But once he made a law, he could not break it. He had to throw his friend Daniel into a den of lions. King Darius said, "May your God, whom you always serve, save you."

All that night the king worried and could not sleep. He was afraid Daniel would become the lions' dinner.

The next morning he ran to the lions' den. "Daniel," called the king, "did your God take care of you?"

"Yes," said Daniel. "He sent His angel and closed the mouths of the lions."

The king was so happy he ordered Daniel be lifted out of the lions' den. The evil men who had trapped Daniel were thrown into the den instead. The lions were so hungry they ate the men immediately.

"All of my people will honor Daniel's God, for He is above all other gods," the king said.

So, for the rest of his life, Daniel helped rule the land of Babylon. And Daniel never forgot to pray.

Story based on Daniel 6.

❖ *Why did Daniel get thrown into the lions' den?*

❖ *How do you think Daniel felt when the king told all the people to worship the true God?*

Prayer:
Dear Lord, help me to remember to talk to You in prayer every day. I'm glad You are always there to listen.   Amen.

There's a Baby in the Feed Box!

Joseph and Mary traveled many long hours. They were going to Bethlehem to pay their taxes.

"I'm very tired, Joseph," Mary said.

"I'll find a hotel room," Joseph said. The city was crowded and Joseph could not find a room. All the hotels were full.

"I have no rooms left, but you can stay in my stable," an innkeeper said. "It will be warm and you can sleep on the hay."

Joseph and Mary went to the stable. While they were there, baby Jesus was born. Mary took the little baby and wrapped Him in cloth to keep warm.

"Let's lay Him in this feed box, Mary," Joseph said.

"Yes, Joseph, a manger is a perfect place to put our baby Jesus," Mary said.

That night shepherds were watching their sheep in the fields. An angel suddenly appeared in the sky and a bright light shone around them. The shepherds were afraid.

"Don't be afraid," the angel said. "I have good news to tell you. God's Son has been born in Bethlehem. You will find the baby lying in a manger."

All at once, many, many angels appeared in the sky. "Glory to God in the highest," they said. "Peace to men on earth." Then the angels were gone.

The shepherds looked at each other. Never before had such a thing happened. Angels had told them of God's Son, born that very night in Bethlehem. "Hurry," the shepherds said to each other. "Let's go see the baby."

So the shepherds hurried into Bethlehem. There they found baby Jesus, just as the angel had said.

They looked at the little baby. "This is God's Son!" they whispered to each other. "What good news the angels brought to us!"

The shepherds left, praising God for all the wonderful things they had seen and heard on this very special night.

Story based on Matthew 1:18-25 and Luke 2:1-20.

❖ *Why did Mary and Joseph have to sleep in a stable?*

❖ *What was special about this night in Bethlehem?*

Prayer

Thank You, Jesus, for loving us so much that You came to the world to bring peace and joy to everyone.

Amen.

Gone Fishin' . . . for Men

The people kept pushing. "I cannot hear what Jesus is saying," a man said, so he pushed a little harder.

"Now I cannot see Jesus," said the woman who had been pushed away.

Jesus knew what the trouble was. The crowd was so large people couldn't see over one another or hear Him. So He got into a boat that belonged to a man named Simon. "Take your boat out a little way into the water," Jesus said.

Simon did. Then, when all of the people could see and hear Him, Jesus told them about God and how God wanted them to live.

When He had finished speaking, He turned to Simon and said, "Take your boat out into deeper water and let down your nets. Then you will get some fish."

Simon shook his head sadly. "We have fished all night and caught nothing. But if You say so, we will try again."

So Simon and his brother, Andrew, did as Jesus said. The nets became so full of fish they began to break.

"Help us!" they shouted to their friends, James and John. So James and John brought their boat over, and soon they had both boats so full of fish that they were about to sink.

They were all so surprised they did not know what to say or do. But Peter fell down on his knees in front of Jesus. "Go away from me," he said to Jesus. "For I am not good enough to be with one like You."

Jesus looked at Peter in His kindly way. "Do not be afraid, Peter," He said. "From now on you will catch men."

The four fishermen believed what Jesus said; nothing was more important now than to be with Jesus. So they left their boats and followed Him.

Story based on Luke 5:1-11.

❖ *What did Jesus ask Simon and Andrew to do?*

❖ *What does it mean to fish for men?*

Prayer:
Dear Lord, help me to be a "fisher of men" and tell others about You.   Amen.

A Basketful of Blessings

One day Jesus and His disciples got into a boat and sailed across the Sea of Galilee. Crowds of people heard where they were going and began walking to meet them. They had heard that Jesus cared for people and healed the sick, so they too wanted to see Him.

When He saw the great crowd gathering, Jesus said to His disciples, "We need some food for these people. Where can we get it?"

They shook their heads. "We do not have any food with us. And it would take a lot of money to buy enough food for this crowd. There are more than five thousand people here. We do not have that much money."

Just then a little boy ran up. He held a basket in his hands.

"I have some food," he said. "It isn't much, but you may have it."

Jesus' disciples smiled. They knew the boy's lunch would not feed very many people. But they turned to Jesus. "This lunch has only five little loaves of bread and two fish," laughed Andrew. "That won't go very far."

But Jesus thanked the boy for his lunch. "Have the people sit down on the grass," He said. Then He prayed and began to break the fish and the bread into pieces. "Give these to the people," said Jesus.

The disciples passed out the pieces of bread and fish. When they came back, they could hardly believe what they saw. Jesus was still breaking off pieces of the little lunch. The disciples kept passing it out until everyone had eaten.

"Pick up the leftovers," Jesus said. "We don't want to waste any food that is left." Quickly the disciples gathered all the food into baskets. "Look!" said one of the disciples. "There are twelve baskets of bread and fish left over!"

"Only Jesus could do such a wonderful thing," another disciple said.

Story based on John 6:1-15.

❖ *How many loaves and fish were there in the boy's lunch?*

❖ *How could one small lunch turn into blessings for the big crowd?*

Prayer:
Dear Lord, help me to share the things
I have with others. Take the things I give
and turn them into blessings for someone else.

Amen.

25

Too Busy to Do the Right Thing

Jesus enjoyed visiting His good friends, Mary and Martha and their brother Lazarus. They lived in a nice home in Bethany, a small town near Jerusalem. And they were always happy to have Jesus as their guest.

One day they heard that Jesus was coming to their house. They hoped He would stay, have supper, and rest for a while.

When Jesus got there, He did agree to stay. Martha was so happy that she hurried into the kitchen and began to prepare a big feast. "I will bake fresh bread and cakes, and roast a leg of lamb," she told herself.

But Mary stayed with Jesus. She wanted to hear Him tell about God and how God wanted people to live their lives.

At last Martha came into the room where Jesus and Mary were sitting. Her face was hot and red, and she looked cross.

"Jesus," she asked, "do You think it is fair for me to be doing all the work while Mary sits in here doing nothing? Tell her to help me."

Jesus shook His head sadly. He knew Martha loved Him and wanted to be kind to Him. And He knew that the work had to get done.

But in His kindly way Jesus said, "Martha, you are making yourself tired doing a lot of things. But being with Me and learning about God is more important. That is what Mary has chosen to do. Why don't you come and join us?"

Story based on Luke 10:38-42.

❖ *What did Mary do that was different from what Martha did?*

❖ *How can you listen to Jesus?*

Prayer:
Lord, help me to listen and learn about You.
Thank You for teaching me Yours ways
through Your Word—the Bible.   Amen.

The Tax Collector's up a Tree!

Zacchaeus was a very rich man. But nobody liked Zacchaeus because he was a tax collector.

"He takes money from us," they said. "He gives some of it to the Romans who rule over us. And he keeps some for himself."

"He cheats," others said.

One day Zacchaeus heard people shouting in the street. "What is happening?" he asked.

"Jesus is here!" they said.

Zacchaeus wanted to see Jesus, too. But he was too short to see over the other people. Then he had an idea. He ran down the road to a big sycamore tree. Zacchaeus climbed up into the tree and sat on one of the big branches. Now he would be able to see Jesus.

The crowd came closer and closer to the tree. Then he saw Jesus. "How tall and strong He looks," Zacchaeus thought. "I know He would never cheat people like I do." Zacchaeus began to wish he could talk to Jesus.

When Jesus came under the tree, He stopped. Then He looked up at Zacchaeus.

"Zacchaeus," said Jesus. "Come down. I want to go to your house today."

Zacchaeus was so happy. He could hardly believe what Jesus had said. He jumped down from the tree and ran to Jesus.

But the people who were with Jesus began to complain. "Why is Jesus going to a sinner's house?" they asked.

Zacchaeus felt sad because of all the cheating he had done. He looked at Jesus. "I'm sorry for what I have done," he said. "From now on I will give half of my possessions to the poor. And if I have cheated anyone, I'll pay back four times what I took."

Jesus smiled. He knew that Zacchaeus meant what he said. "Your repentance pleases God," said Jesus. "This is the very reason God sent Me—to help people like you find salvation."

Story based on Luke 19:1-10.

❖ *Why did the people dislike Zacchaeus?*

❖ *What made God pleased with Zacchaeus?*

Prayer:
Lord, show me the things that I do that do not please You. Thank You for forgiving me when I tell You "I'm sorry."   Amen.

Jesus Is Alive!

It was early Sunday morning. The sky was dark and the city of Jerusalem was still. Three women hurried down the street. They were going to the tomb where Jesus was buried.

"The whole world seems as sad as we are," Mary Magdalene said to the mother of James and her friend, Salome.

Mary was sad, but she was angry, too. "How could those wicked men put Jesus to death?" she asked.

"They were afraid people would obey Jesus instead of them," the mother of James answered. Then, suddenly, she stopped for a minute. "Who will roll the stone away from Jesus' tomb?" she asked.

"If we can't get into the tomb, how can we put our spices on Jesus' body?" asked Salome.

But the women did not have to worry, for when they came to the tomb it was already open! An angel sat on the big stone beside it. It was like looking at a bright light, for the angel's face shone and his robes were glistening white like snow.

"Do not be afraid," the angel said to the women. "Jesus is not here. He has risen from the dead, just as He said. Come and see the place where He used to lay. Then go tell the disciples the good news that Jesus is not dead."

The women were still afraid, but they were excited, too. They turned and ran back the way they had come.

"Jesus did rise . . . just as He promised," one of the women said.

And on the way they met Jesus. He greeted them in His kindly way, and they fell down and worshiped Him.

Jesus said, "Go, tell My friends that I will meet them in Galilee."

It was the happiest day for all the world!

"What wonderful news we have to tell!" the women cried. "Jesus is alive! Jesus is alive!"

Story based on Matthew 28:1-10 and Mark 16:1-8.

❖ *What did the three women expect to find when they reached the tomb?*

❖ *What did Jesus do that no one else could have done?*